AF406109

For Annmarie

Copyright ©2025 Cindy Bazor

All rights reserved. No part of this book may be reproduced, stored in a retrieval system in any form or by any means, electronic, mechanical, photocopying, recording, or otherwise, without the written permission of the publisher, except where permitted by law.
To request permissions, contact the publisher at door3press@gmail.com

ISBN: 979-8-9933325-1-2

Door 3 Press
Door3press.com

MADE BY GOD'S HANDS

Written and Illustrated by

Cindy Bazor

Darkness,

emptiness,

and nothing in sight,

when God opened his hands and out flowed light.

He sprinkled the stars into the sky,
and hung the moon for you and I.

God molded the earth to make mountains steep,

and filled the oceans with water deep.

He planted the land with green plants and trees,

then put fish into the seven seas.

God covered the land with roaming beasts,
and let loose birds to fly
north, west, south, and east.

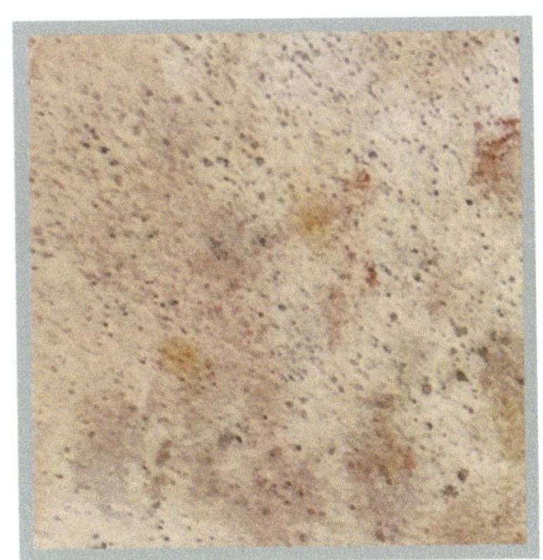

God formed man from dust and his own breath,

then finally laid His hands to rest.

Dear Reader,

Thank you for reading my book. This was a long journey and learning experience for me, from the idea years ago of adding illustrations of God's hands to the creation story, to the process of self-publishing. I've always believed that God is behind all creation, and that He is the Master artist, designer, crafter, and maker!

'Soli Deo Gloria'
Glory to God Alone
"Not to us, O Lord, not to us, but to your name give glory, for the sake of your steadfast love and your faithfulness!" (Psalm 115:1)

Author and illustrator, Cindy Bazor

Cindy is a recently retired high school art teacher. She has completed various types of commissioned artwork and enjoys taking photographs while hiking and traveling. This is her first book. She lives in southern Illinois with her husband, Steve, where they raised two sons and are now proud grandparents.

www.ingramcontent.com/pod-product-compliance
Lightning Source LLC
Chambersburg PA
CBHW042037130726
48010CB00025B/317